Prai
If You Can Make It

This book demonstrates, like few ever have, the value of first-person storytelling as a critically important element in the education of young people. The story of Sam Harris has directly touched the lives of thousands of school children who will be better adults because of the values they have learned from him.

Dr. Christopher Koch – *Illinois State Superintendent of Education*

Sam is a miracle…the miracle is how Sam withstood the full force of the world's worst outpouring of evil without losing his humanity. Sam is a miracle because he was witness to unspeakable, unmanageable horror, and in place of vengeance and hate, he filled his heart with compassion and loving-kindness. Would that all mankind could learn from Sam.

Richard Kaufman – *Psychiatrist. Child and Adolescent Psychiatry, Division of Psychiatry, Emeritus, University of Chicago.*

Sam Harris is proof that one life can produce change in the lives of everyone they touch, no matter what their ethnic heritage. His story is remarkable for what it says about the goodness in the human spirit, and especially for how the message translates so directly to the consciences of young people of all backgrounds.

William Delgado – *State Senator 2nd District, Chairperson, Senate Education Committee*

What is justice? What are the things that we consider good in the world? Mr. Harris, by telling his story to children in their formative years, helps all of us understand the choices we have made in life. He has chosen the path of forgiveness, despite the immense wrongs done to him, and that choice has clearly affected the children who have heard him. Thank you, Sam Harris, and thank you, Ellen Palestrant, for bringing to us this book of hope and immense humanity.

Linda Chapa LaVia – *State Representative 83rd District, Chairperson, Elementary and Secondary Education Committee*

The story of little Szlamek Rzeznik—who we all know as Sam Harris—never fails to bring tears to my eyes. What is so remarkable is how important his story has been to the many schoolchildren who have tasted the evil of the Holocaust, and yet emerged from that experience with a sharper sense of humanity because of him. This book is a must read.

Dr. Ronald Perlman – *President, The Center: Resources for Teaching and Learning*

If You Can Make It Mr. Harris...
So Can I

Edited and compiled by
Ellen Palestrant

Letters from Students to Sammy, Child Survivor of the Holocaust

Sammy the Journey Productions
sammythejourney.com
SocanIfoundation.com

In memory of David Phillip Harris,
Beloved son of Dede and Sam Harris.
Brother of Julie and Jeff Kreamer,
Uncle of Jessica and Jeremy.
1968–2013

Introduction

By Ellen Palestrant

Sam Harris, a child survivor of the Holocaust and the instrumental force behind the creation of the Illinois Holocaust Museum and Educational Center speaks to thousands of people every year relating his story and bearing witness to the Holocaust. He also visits schools and speaks to thousands of school children. Many of these students write letters to him after hearing his story. Sam has told me how precious these letters are to him and that he has kept them all. Once, he said, a student, who was having a very difficult time emotionally, came up to him after his talk and said:

"IF YOU CAN MAKE IT MR. HARRIS, SO CAN I ."

I knew immediately that those words had to be the title of a book that would comprise excerpts from some of the hundreds of letters Sam had received from these students. I chose, with difficulty (because the letters were so moving) excerpts from close to two hundred letters written by these students from Grade 5 through High School.

Sam Harris has an extraordinary story: At age four, Sammy—Szlamek Rzeznik was restricted to a ghetto in Poland with his family. At age seven, the Nazis lined him up together with his mother, father, four older siblings, and other members of his family, in order to be deported by cattle car to Treblinka, a death camp. His father, having first told little Sammy—Szlamek Rzeznik to hide behind some bricks, then pushed him out of the line towards his sister Sara who was hiding there already. Over the next two and a half years, Sam *hid* in two different concentration camps, because, if found, he would have been killed by the Nazis (children were of no use in the work force) and their collaborators.

There had been seven children in his family once; after the war, there were three left—Sam and two of his sisters, Rosa and Sara, who were also in the same concentration camps as Sammy. They never saw their father, mother, four siblings, grandparents, and extended family ever again. Sam describes his harrowing childhood experiences in his book, "***Sammy Child Survivor of the Holocaust***" and also speaks about his experiences in the documentary, "***Sammy the Journey***" created by Eric Cosh and Ellen Palestrant.

After spending time in an orphanage in Poland, then living with his sisters in Austria, Sammy arrived in America in September 1947 together with his sister, Sara. He was twelve years old and hopeful about the possibilities awaiting him. Even though he knew nobody in the USA, and did not know what was in store for him, he was excited about what the future held. This optimism is so much part of Sam Harris' upbeat personality, and, as you will see from the excerpts from these letters written to him by students who had heard him speak, his positive thinking is infectious and inspirational. As one student commented in a letter: *"I would rather talk to you than any football or baseball player that ever lived. You taught me to never hate because hatred never solves anything."*

In the USA, Sam lived in an orphanage and foster homes before being adopted by Dr. Ellis and Mrs. Harriet Harris in April 1948. He was no longer Szlamek Rzeznik but Sam Harris—an American boy—and that was just what he wanted to be. Sam now had his own room in a beautiful house in Northbrook, Illinois—a far cry from the barracks of the concentration camps. He also had a new sister, Susan. Two weeks after being adopted and only seven months after his arrival in the USA, Sam wrote a letter in impressively good English to his only European cousin who had survived the Holocaust and who now lived in Palestine:

April 24, 1948

Dear Chaskel,

I received your letter of March 30, 1948 and I was happy to hear that you are well.

Now I have a new family. April 10th I came to live with Dr and Mrs Harris and their daughter Susan who is 8 years old. We couldn't find a family to take both of us, so I am now their son. And Sara will soon find a good home.

My address is 7 Hickory Lane, Northbrook, Illinois. This is a small town about 20 miles north of Chicago. The homes are not close together, it almost looks like a farm with woods all around it it is very pretty. I have my own room and a new bike which is a part of my birthday present, and I ride it to school. The school is very good and I already have lots of boy friends. We heard from Vienna they are all fine. My new family love me very much and I love them very much too. Please take care of yourself and (write) to us often. I'm forgetting Polish so please write carefully. The Jews in America are worried about Palestine. They are trying to help by sending more money, and by asking the government to do the right thing for the Jews. We pray you and Hadassah are safe and well. We know how hard it is for you now and that you can't write often. You don't have to write to both of us as we will send your letter to each other.

My new Mother and Father send you greetings and pray for your good health and safety.

With love to you and Hadassah

Samuel Reznik
Harris
(this is my new name)

The letter was returned to Sam a few days later. The wording on the envelope read: **"Return to Sender. Service Suspended, because of the War."** Thirty years later, Sam returned this letter to his cousin, Chaskel, now living in the State of Israel.

Sara was adopted by another family in Chicago. Over all these years, they have remained close. Rosa, who recently passed away, lived in Austria but would visit them in the USA, and they would visit her in Austria.

Mrs. Harris kept a record of Sam's progress for the social worker. She started it soon after he came to live with them and completed it about a year later when he was thirteen. Her candid observations, which I have included in this book, offer insights into Sam's development:

Spring—1948

Sam came to live with us April 10, 1948. Along with his personal belongings, he brought with him a pair of white mice for which he had great enthusiasm. He unpacked his clothing with dispatch, showed us his few treasures and pictures brought from Europe, gave to Susan little things he didn't want, and when he was finished, gave me his two suitcases with instructions to throw them out because he never wanted to see them again. He definitely was locking his door to his past. Our neighbor's son, Tom, had been told of Sam as an addition to our family. They would be in the same room in school. The whole class had been prepared for the new boy. Tom came over almost immediately and the 2 boys quickly became friends. They had many interests in common. After a weekend of playing together, Tom was waiting for Sam at school the first morning with all the boys in the class. They greeted Sam warmly. He hit a home run in the baseball game by the end of the day. He was "in".

His social adjustment to his school and schoolmates was as easy as that. The people in town were stunned with the idea of a refugee boy in their midst and they opened their hearts to him in a simple and sincere manner. He in turn was poised, beautifully mannered, friendly and out-going. He charmed everyone, friends, and family, by his applicability, his adult social graces and control. His wide variety of interests, his alertness and his easy manner of adjusting to personalities and situations impressed everyone. He was the center of attention and discussions.

However, he was too perfect, too controlled, he is constantly adjusting himself, jockeying as if it were, to everything. He needed desperately to become a child.

It didn't take long to discover that his knowledge of the English language was very meager. At school and at home, it became apparent that he had a good facility for covering up his lack of vocabulary. He had pretended to understand for so long and so well, that he not only fooled everyone around him, but even had convinced himself that he knew quite a bit. In fact, in the beginning, there was little he didn't feel he could do. He was constantly feeding his ego with exploits of his ability, in any line, and we recognized how hard he was trying to build himself up in our eyes and his.

It took concentrated effort to convince Sam that one must work for what one gets whether it be out of books or on a job. He is bright and had learned easily and well up to this point. This was especially true of his schooling in Europe. He did well with little effort. He had to learn how to study, how to think things through for himself. He had to learn how to look up words. He found it hard to believe we wouldn't help him. With his eyes, ears, and brain, he finally mastered the fact that unless he did the work, he wouldn't benefit. He had never learned to carry that kind of responsibility.

He was at a loss at first if every part of every day wasn't planned for him. Despite his many hobbies and his abundant energy, if he was faced with free spare time alone, he was miserable. He wanted to be told what to do and when. Also, if he had a choice to make about anything involving a discussion on his part, he was incapable of making that decision.

His bed symbolizes some kind of comfort and security at such times if he was under stress of any kind. He was very apprehensive in regard to medical exams. We had his eyes checked and he was so upset by the procedure that he went to bed as soon as we came home, in the middle of the day, for comfort.

During that first summer, his control broke once. We were all sitting in our bedroom one Sunday morning, when Susan following some conversation I can't recall, blurted out to Sam, "this isn't your mother. She's mine, your mother and father are dead." He became very red, we were all speechless. Not too quickly, he went to his room. As he didn't come out, I went in. He had been crying and he burst into hard sobs, saying, "that is cruel. I can't forgive her, I want to forget all that." I tried to comfort him and later his dad convinced him that Susan was terribly sorry and that it was still hard for her to share her family, and they made up.

He hates it if anyone refers to his memories in the family circle or if they ask him about Europe. He wants to believe terribly that there was never anything before this.

A year has passed now and much improvement in Sam and the family relationships generally is apparent. He has grown 5 inches, is straight and strong. He is a beautifully coordinated boy, physically. He loves sports and plays every game with skill and enthusiasm. He really is blessed in this respect for it has paved his entrance into every activity. He is in demand because of his skill. He has learned to study and take responsibility for his schoolwork. His report cards have been good, his teachers think he is a fine valuable member of the group. We feel he could do better scholastically because he doesn't spend too much time studying. He reads little, mainly because active sports are so important to him.

Sam is a leader in his class. He is always being elected to some office, being given responsibilities. He is also very popular with the girls who think he is a good dancer. He loves good times, gaiety, fun. He has a real zest for life. He has become a Boy Scout and brings to it the same enthusiasm and sense of responsibility. Here again his desire to excel has made him a fine scout.

Susan and Sam appear to like each other very much. They tease, quarrel a little, rough-house and generally have fun together. They were too nice to each other at first. I

*think they still don't quarrel or pick at each other as much
as brothers and sisters perhaps do. We think they are even
now, a little careful of each other. Sam does control in this
regard more than Susan. Susan, do you like me or hate me?*

*I think that we have gradually come to accept Sam as a
regular member of the family and ties of love and affection
have grown where we frequently forget that he has only been
here a year. However, I don't believe feelings of acceptance
are complete, on our part, or his. He is still a little wary and
careful, still watches our reactions quite intently, for cues.*

*On the other hand, he is much more relaxed, often
forgets his manners, even is disobedient and forgetful. He is
much more interested in his contemporaries than in adult
visitors now days and quite absorbed in himself and his
activities. This leads us to believe he's made strides in turning
into a typical adolescent American boy.*

Sam, indeed, embraced his life in the USA. He
enthusiastically enjoyed the freedoms he now had, the
generosity of the society around him, the fact that he
was allowed to try almost anything that challenged or
interested him, and there was always the chance of suc-
ceeding in the areas he had selected. He drew upon the
same courage that had helped him in the camps, but,
this time, that courage was accompanied by optimism,
not fear. In America, Sam now had the possibility of
becoming anything. After being in this country for about
three-and-a-half-years, he wrote an essay about America
in his almost-fluent English:

Highlight Spot of My Life.

America is indeed the best place on earth. Most people born in America may not think the same way I do because all the freedoms come to them as natural as breathing. I being born in Europe and living there through the war, have a different respect for Democracy as being practiced in the U.S.

Not until about three and a half years ago did I know what Democracy was. Then the day came. I moved to this free country. This was a complete change for me in the way people lived and the language they spoke. In all the countries I have been, including Poland, my birthplace, Austria or Germany, did the people move so freely and live in such modern countries. When still on the harbor ship, the **Ernie Pyle**, *I starred at all the million lights which brightened the night. Between the huge buildings and our ship on the water there lay a little island on which rested the Statue of Liberty. Even not knowing yet what this huge statue was, I stared at it with great interest. Then I questioned. When I realized what it symbolized that much more my eyes brightened with freedom and my heart beat like the drums of peace.*

Now I have lived in this heaven for three and a half years and still I think of these first visions of real human life which all the people all over the world should some day experience. My heart, I should hope, will never let me forget the sight of liberty my eyes saw on the first night in America. "God bless America." (1951)

It took Sam many years to merge his American self—Samuel Harris—with the little, European boy in hiding, Szlamek Rzeznik—Sammy—who could have been killed at any moment by the Nazis—grown-ups—prepared to even kill children because they were too unproductive to work in the camps.

Largely, because of the influence and encouragement of his wife, Dede, he eventually integrated his past with the present: Sam and Sammy united. Dede helped Sam recognize how impressively courageous the young boy, who had hidden in concentration camps in Poland, had been. Although Sam had become connected with Sammy again, he also knew, instinctively, that in order to continue to live the life he now had with his habitual joy and positivity, it was healthier for him to detach to some extent from the little boy, just as he always did from his physical pain (a result of years in the camps and accompanying starvation) otherwise there was the danger of dwelling interminably on the horrors of his past, on the murder by the Nazis and their collaborators of his parents, grandparents, four older siblings, cousins, friends—just about everybody he had known and loved. He now had a wonderful wife, children, grandchildren, family and friends—a full and rich life; the Nazis had not terminated him.

Today, while keeping the gifts of freedom and seemingly endless possibilities at the forefront of his life, Sam continues, simultaneously, to honor the memories of the millions who were murdered. He was instrumental in building a 65,000 square foot Holocaust Museum and Educational Center in Skokie, Illinois of which he is President Emeritus. Dede, a sculptor and welder, works together with Sam on Holocaust education. Sam gives speeches to thousands of adults every year. He also stresses the importance of not hating.

Then there are the children he has visited over many years—thousands of them at different schools. Sam says: "One-and-a-half million children didn't survive. I made it. I owe it to them to tell their story." Sam, who would have been killed by Nazis and their colluders if he was found while hiding in either of the two concentration camps, feels compelled to help children today for though they do not face the horrors he did as a child, they, too, need protection from the bullies of the playgrounds (who could grow up to be dictators in their own domains) or from the stresses of difficult family or financial situations some have to deal with—or from their own malaise— habitual discontentment. Kids quickly relate to the *Sammy* in Sam—the seven-year-old boy hiding in concentration camps and the twelve-year-old boy who came to America with dreams of a happy future. They find Sam's positive, *I-can-do-anything* personality, combined with the young Sammy's ability to survive, enormously motivational and encouraging. They look at themselves and ask: "Could I have done that?" "Well, maybe…"

Sam's talks at schools are truly inspirational. They make a difference to the lives of these children. For many, they are turning points as evidenced in the thousand of letters he has received from them. I have selected excerpts from some of these letters to show the impact Sam has had on children. In his speeches, he begins with something like *"I will tell you of a little boy called Sammy, who, from age four to age nine and a half, witnessed some of the horrible crimes of the Holocaust."*

Sam then tells the students about how wonderful his life had once been in his hometown in Deblin, Poland, where he was engulfed in the love of his whole family. Those were indeed halcyon days for a little boy, but then came the war, loss of almost everyone he loved and knew, terror and starvation. He tells them about the terrible atrocities committed by the Nazis and the many times he miraculously escaped death. Yet, Sam is restrained when he tells them about the horrors he had endured—strong and self-possessed. He jokes, when appropriate, with the students, and encourages them to never give up hope for they can be anything they want to be. He stresses the fact that they should never give up. They *can make it* if they try. Life presents opportunities. Just look for them.

Sam has an innate ability to relate to kids. They see him as a friend—*Sammy*. Some call him by that name, Sammy, as exemplified in their letters. Sam is intergenerational. He brings out the best qualities in kids—their intrinsic kindness and concern. They are in awe of his courage.

I loved all the letters because they were so genuine. They express the students' needs to be given values to emulate that truly resonate with them. These are preferable to the ones given by the intensely marketed role-models they are expected to follow. Through Sam's talks and the students' responses, we can see that deep within the children resides their very own qualities of courage and decency—values that are within reach. And we have to ask ourselves how we can stop this continual bombardment of misinformation: only *things* that are purchased are of value and *image is everything*. These letters tell us that these students readily recognize in Sam something far more worthwhile—and more achievable—than what is being offered to them by the media and the marketers.

Children are being interfered with. They should be allowed, indeed encouraged, to find within themselves, the qualities of bravery, courage, kindness, responsibility, empathy, and self-reliance which they evidently gravitate towards considering their reactions to Sam's stories. They don't have to go to a store or go online to purchase their personal abilities because these qualities already reside within them. They don't need media or illusory role-models to tell them what they *need* to purchase in order to succeed in life. These letters, undoubtedly, show us that there is innate goodness and caring in the students. Being brave is not only a quality that the students really admire but is also something within the scope of possibility for them. They, too, can be brave.

Too many people (kids included) cling to past grievances. Sam is an example of someone who does not. Kids, in their letters, admire him for that, too. They are impressed with the fact that he does not hate Germans, for example, or any other nation. He does not gravitate to collective demonization—the tool of the Nazis and their willing followers. The kids see in Sam a *great man*, someone whose embrace of the good qualities in people is admirable. Yes, they want to be like him.

The empathetic ability of these students is apparent. Many put themselves in Sam's shoes and wonder if they could have survived the horrors he had to endure. Sam also challenges kids to think about survival. Could they have survived the terrible deprivations and fear to which he was subjected? They are not sure they could have. Yet, they seem to realize that they can survive their present day, perceived or real difficulties, and thrive as Sam has done.

So the big question for most kids is could they have survived hiding in a concentration camp? Most feel they wouldn't have, but then it is only when people are in survival mode that their potential ability to counter incredibly frightening situations kicks in. The kids project themselves into Sam's situation and ask themselves: What if? How would I do? What would I do? Would I survive? How? It also makes them realize that what they complain about is often trivial by comparison.

Sammy was cruelly robbed of his family—and his childhood. Kids of today are being robbed of their childhood, too, although certainly not in the sadistic, incomprehensibly vicious way that Sam had been, but in ways that are becoming increasingly harmful to their development, in ways that are unacceptably self-serving to marketers. Kids are being relentlessly influenced by cynically manufactured "brands"—role-models—who, sadly, are often, simply illusions—part-people. Kids are being made to become *otherselves* traveling so far from their own selves, that they have lost sight of their own potential—their own marvelous, pure emotions and intrinsic, unfettered values. The marketers of goods promising social success, desirability, fame and fortune, have told them endlessly that the more material things they purchase, the more they will be like this or that celebrity—individuals who are generally nothing more than promotional figments. And, sadly, what happens in childhood, could continue in adulthood. These children often become adults who are so removed from their own originality, individuals who become collectives, modeling themselves on what they have been fed by the media and popular culture. Kids are being robbed of being *themselves*.

Even worse than the seemingly non-ending marketing of material values are the messages of hate for the *other*—in the name of *virtue*—instilled by dictatorial leaders (political, religious, or a combination of both) in many societies and countries. Children, who have the intrinsic potential to care about others, are being indoctrinated to hate instead.

I feel in this book, I am documenting the capacity kids have to experience real caring emotions and empathy. It's a great pity that their real selves are usurped by the hegemony of the media or dictatorial leaders. Please, I want to tell them:

LEAVE OUR KIDS ALONE. JUST LET THEM BECOME WHO THEY ARE MEANT TO BE. DO NOT FORCEFEED THEM TO BECOME HOSTAGES OF CYNICAL MARKETING OR POLITICAL STATEGIES.

The kids are inspired by Sam's courage and heroism. This is the kind of role-model—as opposed to a *role-muddle*—they need and crave. A disservice is being done to our kids. Kids are impressed and grateful that Sam actually takes the time to visit schools and educate people. They are grateful that he feels that they are important enough to visit, to talk to, and to share his experiences with them. And, the fact that he takes time out of his busy schedule to do just this, means they *must* be worthwhile.

Sam knows he can connect personally with students because that twelve-year-old boy who came to the United

States eager to become Americanized, is always within summoning distance for him. He can become that excited boy again and the students perceive this. So many children have problems today, whether it is loss of a family member, divorce, abuse, alienation, or financial worries, and when they learn from Sam's talks the circumstances he was forced to endure, and the fact that, despite all of this, he emerged victorious, they line up to both confide in him, and also to tell him that he is their hero. They realize that if Sam Harris could make it, so could they.

Sam is inspired to continue with these school talks when he learns of the effects it has had on children, for example, one teacher told Sam that after he spoke to the school, a bully came over to her and said he would not be a bully any more. In fact, he wrote an essay condemning bullying.

So kids really get Sam's message. We therefore should never underestimate their capacity for understanding problems and for wanting a better world. It is our responsibility to try to ensure, as much as we can, that they will have this. The gratitude kids feel to be in Sam's presence is immense and palpable. As I read through these letters, I kept thinking how intrinsically nice these kids are and how sad it is that they are being intentionally mislead. Sam helps the students, with whom he speaks, to develop a sense of proportion and a more universal outlook on life. They realize that there are many children and adults who have it much worse than they do, yet succeed in life. Sam gives them hope.

Letters from the students remain Sam's treasured possessions, and he keeps them all. He does, of course, appreciate the many letters he receives from dignitaries. Bill Clinton, for example wrote in 1999:

Dear Sam,

... There will one day come a time when the Holocaust will pass from living reality and shared experience to memory and history, and each of us has a solemn obligation to ensure that this tragedy is never forgotten. By sharing your personal story, you are helping the world heed the lessons of history, and I thank you for speaking out.

Hillary and I send our best wishes.

Sincerely,

Bill Clinton

Yes, Sam knows he must share his "personal story" and bear witness to the Holocaust. He continues to do this despite tremendous odds, both physically and emotionally. While I was working on this book, and Eric Cosh and I were making the documentary, Sam and Dede's beloved forty-five-year-old son, David, died suddenly of a heart attack. The loss has been enormous.

I asked Sam if Eric and I should delay completing the film. This is Sam's emailed response:

We must carry on. Dede and I are determined to continue with our work. It's essential. Recently, I spoke to a large audience. One student asked me how I could cope all these years considering my background of the Holocaust. That was a rather deep question to respond to quickly but there is an image that has guided me through my life and so this is what I told the audience: "I remember that when I was in 7th and 8th grade in Northbrook, Illinois, how, in early winter, when there was a slight snowfall and the first frost, all of us kids went to the top of a nearby hill with our sleds. We then sat on our sleds and down we went. The problem was that at the bottom of the hill, there was a pond that was barely frozen. I noticed that those kids, who went slowly, stopped in the middle and sank through the thin ice, but the sleds that went fast, went right over the pond onto dry land. I applied that image to my life. In fact, I would say it is my life's philosophy: I move fast and therefore do not stop in the middle of the pond. I look ahead with all my exciting activities in my view." This, I will apply to the passing of my dear son David on July 6th, 2013. Dede and I are indeed treading on thin ice but we are moving on with life. I have many talks already booked for this year to give to both adults and children.

Because of our enormous respect for Sam—for who he is as a person and for the work he is committed to doing—filmmaker Eric Cosh and I feel very grateful that we have the opportunity to produce a documentary about his life-story. We believe the positivity of his message needs to reach even more people. One man alone can only do so much. He can't be everywhere but we hope that his story, now, will reach many more people and places. Watching and listening to Sam is truly inspiring.

The following letters reflect the different age groups of the students and their levels of fluency in English. I chose not to correct the spelling or grammar because I felt these errors added to the charm and authenticity of the writers. These letters are written from the heart.

I also chose not to categorize the letters of the students because the different qualities each recognized in Sam, and the variety of accompanying emotions, preclude slotting the letters into artificial boundaries. As you will see, the students' comments flow almost seamlessly into each other creating a kaleidoscope of values that they crave. In turn, I have included my own observations on the thoughts of the students.

I have only included in this book, excerpts from letters of students—5th grade through high school. There is one exception, however: the first excerpt from this collection, was signed by both the students and staff:

Dear Mr. Harris…

First and foremost, we would like to thank you for coming to Latino High School and speaking with us. It was truly an honor to have met such a great person like you. The experiences you shared with us about the Holocaust were truly life-changing. It is inspiring to see the positivity and happiness you spread even after the cruel experiences you went through as a child. You have inspired all of us to push to succeed in life and to believe that anything in life is possible if we set our minds to it. Your experiences made us look at life differently and become thankful for what we have in life. You also taught us about the many horrific acts that were committed in the Holocaust which made us realize the reality of that part of history and how it affected the lives of many men, women, and even children. You left us all with a first account memory. It was a truly memorable moment to have had the opportunity to have you speak to us and with us. We are thankful that you have chosen to speak to us and with us. We are thankful that you have chosen to speak to people across the world about your experiences and educate everyone about the Holocaust. Thank you.

**The students and staff of
Latino Youth High School**

◇◇◇

You are one of the best spirited people I have ever known. When you came into the classroom it took my breath away. I couldn't believe I was finally meeting you! When I first read your story I was soooo excited and I'm really excited to get your book too! What your story means to me is that there is good and there is bad but, just because someone comes from a catholic religion or a christian religion or any other who's done bad does not mean I have to hate them. I get your message and I will spread the word to make sure that something similar to this never, ever, ever, ever happens again. I vow to never stand still and quiet when someone is being bullied. I will stand up for them and make sure that they aren't bullied again. I can take being a good person with a decent amount of friends than being a bully and having 1 trillion friends any day. This is what you are to us, a role model. Thanks and keep on doing what you are doing.

Danusia

◇◇◇

I most likely wouldn't have been able to cope with this like you did. When I read your book I whimpered. You are the most strong and brave person I have ever met and have heard of. Even writing this letter makes me cry. If I did survive, I probally would hate the Germans. The fact that you didn't is incredible. I will never forget you. You have inspired me and you are my role-model. Please share your story and try to make your children tell it for you when you can't.

Julia

I know what you been through. I think you are a very strong man. Every time death has come you have avoided it. Times where you could have died but you are alive. You are a strong man. The strongest man I ever knowed. You are a peaceful and humble man.

Juan

Szlamek Rzeznik I don't know where to start. You are truly an amazing person. There was NO REASON for what you had to face. That should never have happened to you. You are just such a good person. I would spend so much money just to hear you tell your story but to hear you speak for free is awesome. I wish I could say to every Jewish person that was killed that there was no reason for that to happen but I can't.

Will

You are the bravest man ever. If I was you I would have died. I probably would have gave up and died. I would have peed in the bed too if all those bodies were there. You taught me not to hate people.

Michael

It takes a very strong person to live through what you did. Many people would never visit the consitration camp they attended. I don't think I'll ever meet a more incredible person than you. I would rather talk to you than any football or baseball player that ever lived. You taught me to never hate because hatred never solves anything.

Nick

Growing up as a child and watching all those unbearable memories must have been really hard for you. All I want to say is that I am glad you are here now, and that there's people like you that actually care about everyone! I hope you keep passing on your wiseness and some day maybe reach peace.

Damaris

When you told us when your father told you to run and pushed you out of line my eyes were watering up, because it was probabily the last time you saw your father. You probabily didn't get to see the last smile on his face, or tell him that you loved him one last time. That's really sad and I'm really sorry about your family.

Jackie

I'm very privileged to get to listen to your story. You were very funny and intelligent and I think you should continue to tell your story to the youth of America. You're a very gifted speaker.

Jacob

Your story was so inspiring to me. You are an amazing speaker. Normally when we have guests come talk to us there are kids who will rudely talk over the speaker. That was not so during your presentation. Everyone was listening intently to try and hear another piece of your inspiring life story. I really loved the message that you conveyed; always stand up for what you believe in and never give up. I really needed to hear that. Mr. Harris, I cannot thank you enough for coming and speaking at our school.

Piper

The pain you went through was close to unbearable. You're a hero in my book and I appreciate all that you do. Thank you!

Cam

First things first. I want to thank you so much for coming. Your story was so fascinating and inspirational. I can't imagine going through all of that at just 7 years old. You are so lucky and I am so honored to get to have met you. I wish that all the memories from the experience would go away for you. During the story, you told us that you had to hide from the Nazis and that is something I don't know how I would have had the courage to do. Mr. Harris you are an extraordinary man and you are a great example on life. In fact what you said about how there's good and bad people, of any race, that sounded exactly like what I would tell myself. Every word you said was touching and powerful. You are a hero to me and others.

Hailey

◇◇◇

I wouldn't imagine what your sisters must have gone through. I love my brother very much and if anything would happen to him I would want to die. I found it very sad how you never saw your parents after they told you to hide behind the bricks. They saved your life! And I'm pretty sure they loved you very much. As soon as I got home after school, I told my mom your story and she nearly wanted to cry. So did I when I heard your story.

Alexa

I cannot even imagine going through anything you have. My sister is younger and I can't begin to imagine how she would react to something this big. I was amazed to hear that you stayed quiet and didn't move. You were taken away from half of your family with still so much life ahead of you. To hear that you walked out of the house and there was a big pile of dead people, and you knew some of them would have been terrible. I have no idea how I would have reacted in that kind of situation.

Angelika

A thing I learned is get along with your parents, Like don't say "you hate them" because you might not mean it but your mom or/both dad might die you can't take back those words.

Christine

When you were telling us your stories it almost made me want to cry, but I couldn't because I should have been happy to actually see you alive. After everything that happened you are a surviver. When I think about everyone who died because someone didn't like your religion I get so mad and I just want to cry because as Christians I would assume they would have been more caring. I only wish I was there...I would have helped as much as I could. I just want to cry. I am so sorry for everything. You really got everyone's attention because I have never seen my peers so quiet before and sit eagerly on their chairs.

Kimmy

I don't know how you could've remembered your experiences at such a young age. I can barely remember anything from my childhood. I'm terribly sorry that you lost your family other than your two sisters. I think that the memory of you walking outside and seeing a stack of dead people that you knew piled up must've been the most frightening thing in my opinion. Then also pulling out a small girl covered in blood from the pile. I think that you were lucky to have survived considering that you were put in the gas chamber group, the shooting room, and the Nazis found where you were hiding a couple of times. I can't believe the horrors you had to go through.

Chelsie

It must have been hard to be a kid during World War II. Nearly getting killed having most of your family die. I would have went crazy. I send my condolences to your family.

Xavier

Did you miss your mother and father? Because if I was to lose my Mom and Dad, I wouldn't be able to live without them. I still can't believe you lost almost all your family. What your Dad did was really brave of him to push you out of the line.

Heidi

To know that people have actually done that to other people is ashaming. But very encouraging to know that you survived. Also it's nice to know that through all that you still enjoy life and not have all that hold you back. I learned a lot from your story. Like what they did to young kids. How they killed them because they were useless. I also learned that don't let things hold you back from living your life.

Tierra

I know that my life can't compare to what you went through. You are a very strong man because I know if I had to see those bodies along the streets I would cry. I think I would cry if I went through everything you did. I'm sorry for what you went through though. I know my apology won't work for everything that happened but I feel bad. I feel bad because I thought I had a rough childhood but after hearing what you went through I guess I don't have it bad.

Monicah

I am amazed at what you went through and survived. The majority of kids probably would not have been able to handle something like that. I am continually amazed that you survived and stayed off clinical depression, as I need thirty milligrams of Prozac a day to get along. You had shown a strong will to live through the worst of times, in such gravity of peril that is incomparable to anything in the twentieth century. You are doing something noble and important… reinforcing the knowledge in people's minds that it really happened and that these were people, not a story.

J.D.

◇◇◇

I learned one important thing from your visit. You should never give up even if life is hard. I learned that even though you think your life cannot get any worse, you keep on going. I learned that you should not give up even though life seems like it is coming to an end. You should always take at least one more step. It must have been hard for you to lose most of your family. I don't know what else to say, but Thank You. You have changed me by coming here, and I thank you for that.

Jessica

Another lesson you taught me was to take advantage of everything in life because one day it could all be gone. This is an important lesson because now I know how precious things like my family and friends are. Your story was truly eye-opening.

Lisa.

Thank you for talking to the whole 8th grade about your experiences. People need to understand what happened and what the Nazis did to you guys and I think it is really great that you shared what happened to you. I thought it was really interesting and frightening that the only way you survived was by hiding in the concentration camps. When I was six years old I would be living at my house and I could never imagine what you had to go through only at the age of six.

John

In my life, I am going to be so grateful for everything that I have today, because almost everything I have is so much more than everything that anyone had during the Holocaust.

Eric

I felt scared for you when you said you had to hide in order for your life to be saved. When you told us all the stories about how you and your sisters stayed together, it was really touching because my sister and I are really close and I hope she would do the same thing for me. I almost wanted to cry when you told us about the room where you were about to get shot. I don't know what I would have done. I can't put myself in your position because nothing that terrible has ever happened to me. I don't know how to express myself much more and all the feelings I felt.

Lisa

I'm glad you came to our school because you taught me not to take everything for granted because I always do. You also taught me to appreciate what I have because when I go shopping I always get things I'm never going to use. You also taught me to appreciate my parents and siblings because one day they could be taken away from me. If I were you I would never have the courage to say my memories of such a horrible place.

Maria

◇◇◇

Not many people know but I used to wet my bed, too. I've grown out of it now. If I had to walk under dead bodies I wouldn't go to the bathrooms either! When you hid in the concentration camps and in a barn I could visualize it. It was scary and I don't know how you kept from breathing, but it is good you did not. It is so good you teach kids like us what you experienced.

M.

◇◇◇

It was terrible what the Nazis did to you and millions of other Jews. You taught me that I should take advantage of my life because it could be done in a flash.

Karen

Your story of your life made me realize how blessed I am. I can apply this to my life by not taking the things I have and the rights I have for granted. You taught me that even in the darkest of times, if you have a positive attitude you can receive hope and bravery to keep you going.

Nick

During your presentation I was making connections to my life, having to do with the ages of you and your sisters and me, and my brothers. You all must have been so strong to withstand what you did, because I can't imagine it. Even after all you have been through, you are able to find the good in all people. When you said you never leave any food on your plate, I can totally understand why you do so, and think you are entitled to do that after all you have made it through so much. I will always remember your speech today and how much courage it probably took to tell it.

Morgan

◇◇◇

life-changing ◇ > > push to succeed in life
◇ > > a first account memory ◇◇ > you
should continue to tell your story to the youth of America
◇ > ◇ you have inspired me ◇ > ◇ you are
my role-model ◇ > > please share your story and
try to make your children tell it when you can't > ◇◇
you are a strong man > > ◇ the strongest man I ever
learned ◇ > ◇ you are a peaceful and humble man
◇ > ◇ I would have peed in the bed too if all those bodies
were there ◇ > > there was no reason for what you
had to face ◇ > > I only wish I was there...I would have
helped as much as I could ◇ > > I just want to cry
◇ > ◇ I can't believe the horror you had to go through
◇ > ◇ what your Dad did was really brave of him to
push you out of the line ◇ > > I send my condolences
to your family > > ◇ to know that people have actually
done that to other people is sickening ◇◇◇ I guess I
don't have it that bad ◇ > ◇ my eyes were watering up
◇ > ◇ you should not give up though it looks like life is
coming to an end ◇◇◇ I now how precious things
like my family and friends are ◇◇ > I am going to
be grateful for everything I have today > > ◇ you said
about how there's good and bad people of any race > > ◇
you are a great example on life > ◇◇ you're a hero

It still shocks me that you were so little and survived. I learned that I should appreciate everything and everyone who I have in my life. I couldn't believe that if you had to go to the bathroom at night there would be dead bodies. It took great will power for you to survive.

Kelli

I learned not to take things for granted and to be happy for what I have. Your story of your terrifying journey had to be horriable and for you to say that the images will never get out of your head clearly had to be the worst. But when you said what kept you alive was to see what your life had in store for you had to be so powerful. I am very greatful to live where I am today and not have to worry about my life nor my family be taken away.

Ashley

◇◇◇

I have heard of the gassings, beatings and per-sicutions of the Jewish people, it never really affected me that much. I mean, I always felt bad but it really never struck me. When you walked in today you looked like an average guy, doing normal things, talking about every day topics. But the stories you told hit me harder than anything I'd ever heard before. When you spoke I could feel your pain, although I will never know how you must have felt. The thing that struck me the most is that I have a five and a half year old sister. She talks, walks and cries like a normal little girl, but I know there is no way she could comprehend a situation such as yours at her age. Having heard you, my life has been impacted in so many ways I'm still not sure how many. You have taught me more than I could ever have known.

Brian

◇◇◇

I realized I take a lot of things for granted like the little things. I'm able to go out and do and see that you couldn't while you were suffering during that horrible time. When you told us about your whole family being taken away from you it made me realize how lucky I am to have mine with me. I don't know what I would do without them. You're a real hero.

Alex

I am happy that you are alive and well. It was great to have a Holocaust kid speak to us. A lot you had to say was sad for me to imagine. You are right when you said not all Germans are bad. I see that taking anything for granted is a mistake, cause you don't know when it will be gone.

Burt

◇◇◇

When I was four years old I swallowed a quarter. If I didn't get it out soon, I would have died, but your story blows my story away. I just couldn't bear to hear how you lost your father, and trying to hide from the Nazis. I also couldn't bear how you went to two concentration camps. Somehow you survived. I thought a lot of things were bad, but the Holocaust is by far the worst. I will try to change the world like you did and do now.

Lindsey

I look up to you and dream that one day I could be as courageous as you.

J. D

◇◇◇

You are a holocaust survivor you are a hero to so many people including me.

Dan

◇◇◇

Thank you for coming to our school today. It is vary generos of you to give up your time for us. I look up to you as a Jewish hero. Thank you for coming!

Ariel

◇◇◇

I am so excited to see you. I would never have the courage you had when you were a kid. You are amazing.

Grace

◇◇◇

You are my hero!

**Your friend
Ryan**

Super human
A Holocaust Survivor
Marvalous
I am really happy to be seeing a holocaust sur-vivor! I believe that you are all the above and much more!

Mecti

You are young at heart.

Giovanni

It was fun for you at home at one point. But what happened was sad. I feel sorry for all the people you loved and cared about. If I was in your time I say I have not survive but you did that is amazing. You are awesome.

Kienan

I think you are very brave and I am so happy you survived the holocaust.

Ellie

I respect you in all the ways you can think of and thank you.

Pam

How are you? It is amazing that your survived the Holocaust! I bet it was pretty scary. You are a real miracle! I was so happy to meet you.

Amelia

Life was wonderful life was great until the Nazi had to hate. Because you were a Jew they were forced to hate you. You are really nice, you had to pay a price for your belief. It was unfair and unright and all you could do is fight for your life. Without force but with words, your freedom is now forever more.

Sarah

I am really happy that you survived the holocost and I am also happy that you came and took your time to come and talk to us. I know a lot about the holocost because I am Polish and my mom told me about the holocost when I was littler.

Amanda

You started off as a normal boy who loved to laugh and play with toys.

When the Germans came you had to flee

You ran and ran until you were free. Although you had little food,

You kept a great attitude.

You're sister fell in love,

And he helped you through all the above.

Now you are safe despite a cost.

We're glad to say you survived the holocaust.

Christina

You have a great life story. You were very brave especially when you escaped the holocaust.

Jackie

I understand you have been through a lot. I have been through a lot also but nowhere near the pain you have been through. I appreciate your presentation very much, you taught me a lot. Thank you very much.

JD

While very interesting, I wish you had never gone through the terrible ordeal you told us about. No one should have gone through that and I am extremely grateful you survived the Holocaust. It was amazing to me all of the times you went through and that you still wound up coming through and surviving. You showed great courage and bravery in your darkest hours. It takes an extremely strong man to do that. I only hope one day, you are able to sleep well again without bad dreams about the holocaust. You did a great job presenting, thank you very much.

Grace

I am so glad you came to talk to us. It's a great experience to have an actual survivor come to talk to us. It must have been so scary and horrible to go to the concentration camps. Also, when you had to go to that one room with other kids and they told you that they were going to shoot you tomorrow I would be so scared, I would rather not be told that I am going to get shot. It takes great confidence to come and talk about the Holocaust. It was a horrible time in our history, but it should not be forgotten. I am extremely thankful you came to talk to us.

Casey

Thank you so very much for speaking to us 8th graders about your very own story of the Holocaust. Your words were very sympathetic, and I could feel a message in them. Mr Harris, I think you opened many young adults' eyes today. You did mine.

Joey

YOU ROCK! Your speech was very interesting. Your old belt is very interesting. I was very surprised that you didn't break down while speaking. Especially bring back all those memorys.

David

P.S. You Rock even more.

Thank you for presenting to us. It truly left an impression on me. With you being Polish and I being Polish I felt a connection of how our heritage has gone through so much during that time. Your sharing the stories reminded me of my grandfather who was captured by the Nazis and then by the Russians. He finally escaped which reminded me of how your miracle happened and how you got out alive...I thank you from the bottom of my heart for coming.

Chuck

◇◇◇

Thank you for presenting about the Holocaust. I appreciated the speech that you presented. It felt very emotional and painful. Now I understand more about how the Holocaust was a huge crime. This is a once in a life-time opportunity to hear from a Holocaust survivor. This was a thrilling experience

Jason

◇◇◇

Your words affected everyone I looked at. Deep down we are all the same.

Donald

I think you are a very great man! You're such a great role model to people. You're a very nice man and also very funny. It is just so unbelievably great how you survived the Holocaust from going through all the terrible obstacles through your life including some that would've led you to death. It is just so amazing to me.

Hannah

What happened is really a sad thing. I'm German, and I have learned a lot about German history and this is one of the worst actions done by Nazis. I have cousins and an uncle who were soldiers in the Nazi army. They were beaten for not killing Jewish people. The holocost was incredibly horrible.

Jeremiah

It made me sad that you didn't have any pictures when you were little and that you only had a belt. When you told us what you had to endure during the Holocaust, it made me think and what I was thinking was I thought my life was tough. Then I saw what you had to endure was rougher. So I'd like to thank you.

Alex

People are truly touched by your speech. My friend Zac was chronicly sobbing throughout your story.

Will

I imagined the people crying and the people marching down the streets. You are really brave.

Karia

It must have been horrible for all of that to happen to you when you were so young. If I was in that situation I don't think that I would have survived.

John

I think you are a true hero. I think it would take great courage to be able to survive the Hollocast. I will never forget this experience I witnessed today. Your stories really gave me a better understanding.

Lory

Your speech has inspired me to become a better person. Your story is a true inspiration to people who think they have a million problems. It could have been nothing like yours. Hopefully we'll meet again.

Yasmin

I will try to change the world like you did and do now

>>> I dream that one day I could be as courageous as you >>> you are a hero >>> super human >>> having heard you, my life has been impacted in so many ways >>> you are young at heart >>> you're a very nice man and also very funny >>> you're words were very sympathetic >>> I thank you from the bottom of my heart for coming >>> I only hope one day, you are able to sleep well again without bad dreams >>> I am really happy that you survived the holocaust >>> I am happy that you are alive and well >>> you are very brave >>> you taught me a lot >>> you opened my eyes >>> a once in a life-time experience to hear from a Holocaust survivor >>> the holocaust was incredibly bad >>> your words affected everyone I looked at >>> deep down we are all the same >>> if I was in that situation I don't think I would have survived >>> my friend Zoe was chronicly sobbing throughout your story >>> when you spoke I could feel your pain >>> your speech has inspired me to become a better person >>> you made me realize how lucky I am >>> I realized I take a lot of things for granted >>> you are amazing >>> you are awesome >>> you rock

Your story really inspired me. When you were only like four you had to face difficult opsticles. And it must have been really scary. Thank you for wasting your time to tell us your story.

J

I feel sorry that you had to suffer the holocaust as a kid. It is really horrible that you had to suffer through it. You should thank your sister for giving you food in a time of great need. I think you should write a book telling every event you remember.

Harrison

When you were giving us your description of events, like how you and your sisters hid in the barn. I would be so scared. I can tell you that I would not have been able to survive. When they (Nazis) came in to the barn and were searching, I would have just walked out.

Bryce

It was inspiring to know how brave you were in all your near death experiences. You truly are an inspiration.

Casey

I'm sorry for your losses…when you said nobody should forget the Holocaust. It reminded me of 9-11 and nobody should forget.

Michael

◇◇◇

Your story will stick with me forever. Reason being, I learned how much you and your family went through and how much the Jewish people went through.

Jon

◇◇◇

The things that you have been through are incredible. I can't even imagine how hard that experience would be. I am going to read your book. Your time ment a lot to me.

Amanda

I see how it must have been when you were a kid and Nazis had invaded your town, killed friends and neighbors you once knew and how painful it must have been. You are an excellent speaker how you story with many details. Your story sends out a powerful message about how Jews were treated during the Holocaust and about racial segregation.

Chris

I can't imagine what it was like for you to see and live through those horrors at such a young age. It is inspiring to see you become a successful man with a happy life. I know that if I was in that situation I would have given up hope quickly. You are truly a hero for your courage to go through this horrorable thing. This is an experience I'll never forget.

Danny

I want to thank you for not being afraid to tell us about the true experiences that you had—no matter how much it might have hurt you. I also want to thank you for making this somewhat motivational.

Zeba

I think that it was hard because it is not easy to watch your friends, neighbors and family members get killed. It was wonderful how brave you were on surviving all this.

Laura

I think it is a very honorable thing of you to be spreading the word to children, even writing a book, and the new museum. Thank you!!

Jimmy

I could feel the emotions you felt when you went through that time.

Tammy

I really got the jist of what happened during the Holocaust. It's very cool to listen to an actual survivor. I'm sorry to hear that you lived through such hard times. I think that it is people like you that help pass down history, and keep the children in the future educated.

Charlie

All the things that you have experienced and went threw has touched me. I am proud of you. Also that you survived and had a chance to tell us your story.

Andrea

I know that it took great will-power to tell of people close to you dying in front of your face. But I am very greatful that you came and told of your struggles. Thank you soooo much for this great experience.

Aditi

I thought all of your stories were interesting, especially the one about the time when you and your sisters had to hide under the hay while the Nazis looked for you. I would just like to thank you for your courage and perseverance during the war. You are my idol.

Conner

Through your speaking, I've learned the thoughts and feelings of a real survivor through your voice and presence. I really liked when you said you did wrestling and karate...but I liked how you felt you needed to stand up for yourself. I wish a lot of us can also learn from past experiences. I feel bad for your dad. I cannot believe what happened to him. I knew they beat people but what you said gave a bigger picture because it was your experiences and images. You taught me a lot today.

D

Your story of bravery and heroism has inspired us all. If I was in your position, I would of never been able to do all that you did not only for yourself but for others. Also you have experienced some scenes that are too gruesome for the movies, but you were forced to face them in real life. I am sorry you had to experience this.

Erik

I could see everything you were saying in my mind. Your story was very touching especaly when you said that you saw that Jewish man pleading for his life. I don't know how you could of handled it. It was very good of you to have expressed your feelings.

Tyler

P.S. Remember our cool hand shake, where we touched fists.

◇◇◇

In a sense, I could almost feel your pain.

Gunnar

◇◇◇

I also liked it when you said you were a wrestler because I wrestled for Prairie this year (2006-2007) and didn't do so bad for a rookie (12-12) was my record. Overall your presentation was the best I've ever seen and think you are doing what's right by telling people about your experience and what you went through and I think creating a museum is one of the greatest ideas you could come up with, and I'll make sure to check it out.

Cammeron

◇◇◇

If everyone were just a little bit more like you, the world would be an incredible place. Your willingness to educate others shows how truly amazing you are.

Burton

I am amazed to think that a man who survived the Holocaust and still walks around with a smile was talking to me. You made me realize how much I take for granted in life. I realize that the last thing you want is anger towards all Germans and I know everyone respects and agrees with your request. I'm touched that after all you have been through, you still care so much. I believe your point is not to make people feel sorry for you, but just to acknowledge and realize that not only did the Holocaust happen, but you were there. You've taught me to enjoy everything, because at any moment it could all be gone. Your story will live on forever.

Jeremy

You inspire me and I look up to you in every single way. Whether it's to keep going and not give up or to think about how lucky I am to have a great life.

Lauren

You should be so proud of what you've done and what you are doing. You are a great role model. You'll always be in my heart.

Allison

You are an amazing person. I think it is amazing that you could live through all of that and be so very positive. I really admire you for that.

Alex

I am amazed at your life and what you went through. You are truly very strong and good-willed, even at an early age. You truly are a hero as well as your two sisters who helped you.

Yvonne

Your stories made me realize how lucky I am to be living with everything I need and going to sleep with a full stomach.

Celia

I think it was very cool about all of the things that you went through surviving. When you were explaining your story I was thinking, wow, Mr. Harris you're like a legend if you actually survived all the stuff you went through.

Sammie

You have truly inspired me to believe that anything is possible and that I can overcome any obstacle. I am a teenage mother and I always believed that having a baby at such a young age would interfere with my dreams, but you have taught me to realize that anything that I can believe, I can achieve. I was so fortunate to have met such a wonderful and inspiring person like you. It takes such courage and strength to speak of such a tragic time. You have truly taught me to speak for what I believe in and to make a difference in the world, just like you have.

Stephanie

I think that no teacher or my parents will ever teach me what you taught me. I have always wanted to do something with my life, but putting it to work and not giving up has been difficult because of what has happened in my life. The things that you went through and the things you have done throughout your lifetime have motivated me to never give up, and for this reason I will never forget your words: "Never give up." Thank you Mr. Harris, you are among my heroes.

Ivan

I'm telling you, most people like you would go in depression forever but you seem so happy and it's great.

Nick

I admire you so much for doing what you do. I wouldn't have the courage to talk about something like that, but to me you're a hero. I would also like to thank you for listening to my story about when I had my daughter. I know you kept asking for a picture so I'm sending you one with this letter. Thank you for coming to our school and may God bless you and your family.

Toni

I was very captivated by what you said, all of it. It's amazing how your wonderful attitude towards life is still here after the horrific events you've experienced. I admire you for the things you've done and the person you've become. I pray our paths will cross again.

M

I'm glad you showed up in our school. You really taught us a lot of things. It must have been hard for you to make that presentation of expressing yourself. I am happy to see a holocaust survivor and when I have my children I would remember of you and tell them what you told us and let them know the holocaust did really happen.

D

It's amazing that even after what you have gone through you still have a great sense of humor. It was truly an honor to have been in the same room as you Mr. Harris.

David

I could feel the emotions you felt when you went through that time ❯◇❯ I could almost feel your pain ◇❯❯ I could see everything you were saying in my mind ◇❯❯ how lucky I am to have a great life ◇❯❯ if everyone were just a little more like you the world would be an incredible place ❯◇❯ it's very cool to listen to an actual survivor ❯◇❯ it's people like you that help pass on history and keep children in the future educated ◇❯❯ your story will stick with me forever ◇❯❯ your story sends a powerful message about racial segregation ◇❯◇ I realize that the last thing you want is anger towards all Germans ◇❯❯ you still have a great sense of humor ❯◇◇ you still care so much ◇❯❯ it took great will-power to tell of people close to you dying ❯◇◇ this is an experience I'll never forget ◇❯❯ we shouldn't give up ◇❯❯ I like how you felt you needn't to stand up for yourself ◇◇❯ I am proud of you ◇❯◇ you will always be in my heart ◇◇◇ you are truly very strong and quick-witted ◇❯❯ you have taught me to realize that anything that I can believe in, I can achieve ◇❯❯ I look up to you in every single way ❯◇◇ you are a great role model ◇❯❯ you're like a legend ❯◇❯ you are my hero

Yesterday when you came to our school Latino Youth High School to talk to us about your past experiences during the holocaust I know you changed everybody's live in a way you did. We had never met such a courageous person who is able to talk about a horryfing past, yet not feel hate for anyone. I'm really glad you came to our school to talk about your experiences which really changed my views of what happen in the holocaust.

Aldeu

Well it was nice meeting you. I mean that I couldn't actually believe that we were going to meet somebody that survived the holocaust. But I enjoyed especially you telling us about your experience because I think that gives an inspiration towards people and me that no matter how hard we're put in a situation we shouldn't give up.

Martina

I was very touched by what you said. What I really learned about was the way you said that hatred was bad and that we should not hate someone who we do not even know. Also the way you raised your children so they would not hate either. That is something I will also teach my son. I will take him to the concentration camps and make sure he does know and will always remember what happened.

Maria

I'm so sorry you had to face those terrible events. It was really interesting about the gas chambers. I never knew they had those. It was also interesting how you hid under the straw and they did not find you. I found that hard to believe. I was wondering if they would step on you and find you. You are very lucky you are still alive from all the harsh events you went through.

Adam

I couldn't believe your Dad saved you and your sister by telling you to hide behind an old brick wall. I can't even imagine how it felt to see everyone you know being taken away to the gas chamber to be killed.

Dahlia

Your story was envisioned in my mind. Your story was so emotional. You are the most brave, courageous, fearless person I have ever met.

Samuel

The story you told us was so sad. I feel so sad that your parents died when you were so young. I can see the stories in my head when you tell them. You are one of the bravest people I have ever met.

Steve

Your stories are probably the most interesting true stories I have ever heard. My favorite thing about your life is about your belt. I can't believe it was the only thing of you childhood you had. I was astounded how the Nazis treated you. Also, you are probably the nicest man I ever met. Your wife is also very nice.

Matthew

I'm astounded by how you stayed alive and hid from the Nazis. It must have taken a great deal of courage to overcome your fears and be brave. Even though sharing your childhood memories is tough it needs to be done. Thank you.

Adam

Thank you for coming to my school and giving me a taste of reality. Your storys and experiences really opened my eyes. They made me realize that when I say my life is bad some people have it ten million times worse. I almost cried when you were telling us your storys about how you had to run a far distance just to escape death or how kids had to pretend being dead. I can't imagine myself doing that. Well anyways thanks again.

Paola

◇◇◇

I saw how hard it was to tell us all of the tragic thoughts you have had over the years. I think that you are an inspiration to a lot of kids all over the world because I know how hard it was to write your book. You were strong enough to tell people everything you went through. You got guts!

Kirtan

You got me thinking how we have an easier life than you did. I think I'm actually going to put what I learned today to use.

Ramiro

Hello, I was one of your audience. As I have wondered my whole life the Holocaust topic if there was any survivors left or even a real event, I started growing up and maturing now I know the Holocaust was real, and for you Mr. Harris to come and talk about it makes by opinion 100% more sure that the Holocaust did happen and there is a Holocaust survivor.

Alex

It hit me very hard when you said you were separated from your family because I am close with my grandparents and siblings. So to hear that you never saw them again would have been really hard for me. Thank you again for coming because you really influenced me to be a better person.

Joanna

◇◇◇

I want to tell you how proud of you I felt while I listenend to your story. Not just because you as a child were strong and brave enough to prosper in such a horrid time, but because you were able to withstand retelling the story for our and future generations benefit. I want to tell you that I will hold on to the story of your experiences forever, especially because I wish to help educate others on the subject and to prevent such a horrible thing from ever happening again.

Kristina

◇◇◇

I really respect you and can't believe you went through such horrid things. I don't just respect you for surviving. I respect you for having the will to go around and share your knowledge with people.

Carry

◇◇◇

It's really wonderful that you go around saying your past (when it hurts to talk about this). I want to say thank you for coming to my school and teaching me this. I am bullied in school but I really don't care because I pretend like I don't know them. I don't let them get to me. I'm sorry about what you have gone through. But what I learned from you is that you and all Jews went through a lot of horror. You opened my eyes to this horror. But it's good to know what happened, so we don't repeat them.

Rozzy

I know it must have been hard for you to talk about this, considering that most twelve-year-olds never see the kinds of things you saw during your stay at the concentration camp, and for this reason I am even more grateful that you took time to come here and tell us about it. I hope nothing like the Holocaust ever happened again.

Eddie

We have had a lot of speakers come to our school, but by far, you were the best. It was so interesting to listen to what being in the Holocaust was like and how it affected your life. In our Communication Skills class, we have all been reading novles about the Holocaust but listening to someone who actually witnessed it is amazing. It was such an honor to have you here.

Grace

My favorite story was the one about you stealing the potatos. I think that the soldier who was chasing you did believe what he was doing was wrong.

Christian

I almost cried when you told me about your whole family being lost and the things you saw. I think how lucky you are to survive. I ask myself why didn't that nazi shoot you. Well I'm glad you shared that with me, and your okay.

Dylan

PS. I'm really happy you came.

I think it is really hard to be in a scary place like that especially when you are a kid. I also think it's hard to lose your family in such a terrible way. I think you're a real strong hearted and brave person to be able to talk about the past again.

Min

I am so happy that you have a wonderful life after that nightmare. I'm sorry your family died but at least your two sisters are alive.

Kim

P.S. I like your belt and potato stories

Your speech was great. The experiences that you have gone through were terrible, but it made you a great and intellectual man. The things you spoke of were horrible but you teach and tell about your experiences to kids who don't really know what happened. To have a speaker share about his worst moments that were part of history is a different experience than learning or reading from a book. I thank you for coming to our school. I won't forget.

Jorge

I really think that it wasn't right for the nazis to treat Jewish people the way they did, and I am very glad you made it through.

Jenny

I'm the Lithuanian boy that you talked to after the speech. I found your story truly amazing and nothing but a miracle. Did you ever meet any SS soldiers? If you did how many and how did they look. Please reply as soon as you can. Also could you spell your name before you were adopted.

Rimantas

I thought "oh my God...this is someone who actually lived through these terrors, these are his MEMORIES." I will never know the fear, the hunger and pain you went through. There are a few things I can relate to you though. Your belt is a major factor. I know what it's like to be emotionally attached to an object that if you loose it you go crazy and tear the house apart looking for it. I have a stuffed bunny that was put in my crib before I was even a day old. I can't sleep without him. I feel safe with him. And I believe that's how you felt with our belt.

Jan

I feel soreness for your childhood. How did you find perseverance to move on? Did you ever regret being Jewish while you were in a concentration camp?

Ryan

The thing that I liked most about your presentation was that your eyes told the story. When you talked about hiding behind the bricks I could see how afraid you were and when you talked about the night the Russians came I could see the happiness and relief.

Jason

I had a question in mind but I was sort of shy at the assembly. The question is what was going threw your mind when you herd you guys were free from the consintration camps?

Mayza

I feel so sorry for you that you lost so much when you were young. I think you touched everyones heart when you said all you had was a belt from your childhood. You also mentioned that you should stand up to bullies and not let them scare you and control you is so true because if we have another bully like Hitler the same thing is going to happen again and there is going to be many millions of people dead so we need to stand up for ourselves so this won't happen again.

Michael

You've been through so much. It's like you had an angel watching over you the whole time. You escaped death so many times. You are really changing the world by talking about your experiences. It's like God chose you to be his messenger. Make a difference because the world needs a change.

Monike

I can never think of putting my shoes in yours if we were really to swap lives. What really touched me was your belt story because I've had this special blanket that I got from my grandmother when I was born. My grandmother passed away when I was very little and the blanket she gave me I hold dearly to my heart and that story is very touching to me.

John

Did you ever think there was no God?

Raven

I still don't understand how you fought through it. If I were you I'd be scared out of my mind. Some parts of your speech made me want to cry. It was just so amazing that I could stand in the presence of a survivor. It was so cool to be able to speak to you in person after the speech. My friends and I were even able to give you a hug. This was a moment I'll never forget.

Cate

◇◇◇

Your story was so vivid and detailed that I could envision the whole story in my head. Also, I think it is amazing that you are able to forgive the Germans after everything that happened.

Stephanie

◇◇◇

I am going to tell you that I am very sorry. For everything that has ever happened to you in the Holocaust and the way you were treated I am truly sorry. You are a wonderful person. You are also a very lucky man. You are a walking luck charm. If I were you I would have just wanted to die. I wouldn't have known what to do. You have proved to me that anyone can do anything. You or anybody else should not have had to go through anything like that. I'm so so so so so so so so sorry. I feel great pain for you. No matter what has happened to you, you manage to stay so happy and wonderful. I got the honor of actually shaking your hand and meeting you. You are a walking miracle. You have a lot of greatness in you and are a wonderful, amazing person.

Nakia

◇◇◇

I feel so sad that your parents died when you were so young ❯ ❯ ◇ I feel soreness for your childhood ❯ ◇ ◇ I almost cried when you told me about your whole family being lost and the things you saw ◇ ❯ ❯ I was astounded how the Nazis treated you ◇ ◇ ❯ you are probably the nicest man I ever met ◇ ◇ ◇ your bright outlook on life just brings happiness to a room ❯ ❯ ◇ your stories and experiences really opened my eyes ❯ ❯ ◇ you are the most brave, courageous, fearless person I have ever met ◇ ◇ ❯ when I say my life is bad some people have it ten million times worse ◇ ❯ ◇ I'm actually going to put what I learned today to use ◇ ❯ ❯ you really influenced me to be a better person ◇ ❯ ❯ I am bullied in school ◇ ◇ ❯ you should stand up to bullies ❯ ❯ ◇ if we have another bully like Hitler the same thing is going to happen again ◇ ❯ ❯ I hope nothing like the Holocaust ever happened again ◇ ❯ ◇ I am very glad you made it through ❯ ◇ ◇ you are really changing the world ◇ ◇ ◇ you have proved to me that anyone can do anything ◇ ◇ ◇ you have a lot of greatness in you ◇ ❯ ❯ you are a walking miracle ◇ ❯ ❯ I really respect you ◇ ❯ ◇ it's such an honor to have you here ❯ ◇ ◇ I won't forget ◇ ❯ ◇ that was the most inspirational talk I ever heard ❯ ◇ you got guts

I feel bad that you had to leave your family forever and to never hear or see them again. I think it is amazing that you survived all those effections and found hiding places. God was watching over you and your sisters. I understand what it was like to lose family members. It's just horrible. Sometimes you wish you can see them one last time. I'm glad you and your sisters survived all the way until the end. But I do feel bad for those who didn't make it. I just feel like crying now because it is terrible to think and see and hear what all those people went through and what you went through. I'm glad those Nazis that hurt Germany were punished because if they weren't they could cause even more trouble. I'm glad you are alive today.

Kaitlin

Your life itself taught me more than any text book could. Your life really made me understand hardships. You also inspired me to have hope in difficult times just like you did in the concentration camp.

Mo

◇◇◇

You taught me so much. First off, you taught me that not all Germans are bad, just the Nazi soldiers. You also taught me that hope carries one a long way! I feel so blessed to have had the chance to talk to you. After hearing you speak I immediately came home and shared your brilliant and fascinating story with my family. I wish those stupid Nazis could see how happy and proud you are today. You are one of those people that I hope everyone gets a chance to meet! Your bright outlook on life just brings happiness to a room. Mr. Harris, I want you to know that this was the most inspirational talk I ever heard! It really shows me whatever I reach for I can achieve. I will share your story with my children and my children's children.

Lauren

◇◇◇

It must have been really scary because you would not know what would happen next.

Nikhil

We can see more of the truth from a real life point of view. I know it must be hard to talk about what happened in front of you while you were still a child who wasn't exposed to death or violence. We as an audience can only imagine what you went through. Most of our mind games will not be worth to comparing with your memories. I hope that every time you open your mouth to release your story which so many don't have the opportunity to speak, you feel lighter by telling biographies of so many. My vocabulary is still inexperienced to describe my gratitude. It was a pleasure to have been in your presence. Thank you.

Victor

◇◇◇

You inspired me not to quit when you're trying to learn a new language. Thank you for your visit.

Hasto

I learned a lot. I learned the thoughts and feelings of a real survivor through your voice and presence. I really liked when you said you did wresting and karate. I do not wrestle or do karate but I liked how you felt you needed to stand up for yourself. I wish a lot of us can learn from past experiences. I feel bad for your dad. I cannot believe what happened to him. I knew they beat people but what you said gave a bigger picture because it was your experience and images. Thank you.

Jean-Luc

◇◇◇

I was surprised to see you so happy and smiling after what you went through. Thank you. It was very inspiring.

Daniel

Your story Sammy inspired me because of all your determination to make it through alive. Your words were touching and I know now that my problems are nothing in comparison to the horrific lifestyle of the Jews in the holocaust. I will never forget you and your story.

Sarah

We are all here for you. I know there are bul-lies here. And honestly, I used to be one too. Until Carma stabbed me in the back and it hurt. It was really mean, and that's when I put myself in those kids shoes I bullied and I stopped. Your talk really meant and taught me a lot.

Jon

I'm now very thankful that I have two parents. I am also thankful that I am born in a good time with no war where I live.

Brett

I can't think of anything worse than being in the Holocaust. I'm glad that I got to ask you my question. I'm really sorry that you lost most of your family and you went through that without food.

Shelby

I thought your book is one of the best books I have ever listened to aloud. I picked up that you can make a change in yourself. As a Holocaust Survivor that was a great conversation.

Ethan

I'm fortunate to have parents and pictures of family and vacations. You went through rough times without parents. I have a roof over my head and food. You were very brave and risked your life many times.

Brayden

You made me realize what a nice life I have and how important parents are. I feel horrible and spoiled because I have complained about Van (my brother) having a bigger bathroom and closet than I do, when you didn't have any of those things. You helped me see how important the little things are.

Addison

I feel very fortunate knowing that I have parents and I don't have to go to concentration camps. And, I don't have to feel the pain that you did. I can't imagine going through anything you did! Do you feel like a hero? I would think so. Also, do you feel like you have a gift of some sort? Luck, Speed, Intelegence, knowing that you survived everything?

Joe

When you said that you missed your mom the most it made me think "How lucky am I to have parents." They take care of you and nuture you. You would probably be really hungry if they weren't there.

Reece

It was awful what happened to your family. I am glad that you mentioned that not all Germans, or Polish, or any other country were all bad.

Madeline

◇◇◇

You taught me that the Nazis were terrible people but not all of the Germans were. I will always remember when you and you're sisters would always stick together and would do anything for each other. I will also remember the time when you and you're sisters kept trying to hide and everywhere you went someone would kick you out and that just shows how mean the people were.

Dana

I will always remember when you and your sisters hid in a barn under straw and Nazis came in looking for you. Luckily, you didn't get caught anytime. I will also remember when you were hiding behind bricks so you wouldn't have to go in a cattle car.

Amanda

I will always remember when you told us about dead bodies hanging between the barracks and the toilets. It scared me so much! I will also remember when you told us about all of the opportunities that you didn't take for granted. It made me feel like you really wanted to make the best of your school life.

Emma

I will always remember what your family went through, for now I know how selfish I can be when I get angry at the smallest things, since your family was almost completely murdered.

Elliot

You showed me that miracles do in fact exists. Now I know you're a devout Jew, and I'm a devoted catholic, but don't we have the same God? Didn't Catholithism come from Judaism? I can now truly say that your story is just living proof that our God is capable of miracles.

Chris

When you made the connection between Nazis and bullies, I realized that bullying must be stopped in order to have peace between people.

Danny

You are an amazingly brave man to have gone through that horror, and still wish to enlighten people about all that happened. I will always remember your story and pass it on to my future children.

Maddy

I think it is amazing that you can still tell about your life while remaining composed. I'm very proud of you and I know I'm just a child but you have all my respect.

Jordan

You were very brave and very strong. If I was in that situation I probably would have had a mental breakdown. You are very happy and always have a smile on your face.

Megan

Today was the best day so far. Why you ask? Well, you came to our school and talked about the holocaust. I can honestly say you have opened my eyes. I told all my friends you are someone I admire, and you are someone who inspires me, a lot. After all it is very hard to talk about. I think it is amazing that you actually stuck threw it all, and talked about it. And through out you had a smile on your face, no tears no nothing. When you were talking about your sister I thought "wow two years older than you and she acted like a mom."

xoxo Azra

I recently just lost my dad and am going through a rough time. After hearing how you lost your parents and your peaceful closure showed me that eventually you will move on.

Colleen

I would change my religion for a short time then I would change back. With your expirence that our class read about I think it would be tough to do what you did.

Brady

I realize now that it can be extremely hard without parents, especially after the Holocaust. The concentration camp sounds really scary. I think that it is important to study the past, and somehow prevent something like the Holocaust happening in the future.

Taylor

I really liked your book Sammy. It gave a lot of information about the Holocaust and how you survived and lived. It must have been hard to hide under the blankets and other stuff. It is really cool that you still have your belt. I bet you wish that you still had your own star and some family pictures.

Janae

Thank you for letting me talk to you. I feel sad that you had to go through that but happy you are still alive. I am sorry about your parents and the others you have lost. But you still have the time to talk to us kids that is so cool.

Jordon

I really did not know much about the Holocaust but when I talked to you and read your book I learned how hard it was. I could not imagine how hard it would be without your parents.

Kash

I like that your not afraid to tell the past and what happened because we need to know, all of us.

Stephanie

You taught me to be grateful for what we have and that also be grateful that we are not in the Holocaust. You also taught me how bad it could be back then and how lucky you were to survive.

Natalia

You taught me that it was a miracle that many people, including you, had survived the Holocaust because of all the dangers that were around. You also taught me that the Holocaust was a real event, not something people want to avoid writing and talking about. I will remember you showing us a piece of barbwire that surrounded the concentration camp that you were in. I will also remember you telling that not all the Nazis were bad.

Emily

Something I will always remember from your presentation is how you had to run outside the fence to steal the potatoes. Also, I will remember the story of when you and your sisters were hiding in the barn. The Nazis came to search, but they didn't find you. You and your sisters were very lucky.

Mark

Honestly, I was surprised that you were so young when everything broke loose around you, and you still managed to survive. It must have been too terrifying; I can't imagine being there when the Germans attacked Poland. I hope that you will continue living a happy life, as you truly deserve it after experiencing the Holocaust.

Peter

This was the first time I had heard a child Holocaust survivor speak and the first time that I would ever imagine being spoken to about the event with a positive outlook. Your attempt to show the Nazis that you were alive and happy was truly one of the most memorable parts of your speech. Most people would not think to have the same opinion, because the Holocaust was such a distressing occurrence. I appreciate you sharing your story with me because I can imagine the difficulty that must have come upon you after remembering such tragic memories and sights. The fact that you shared your story made me realize the importance and significance of telling other people about it, because if you did not then people would not believe that it actually happened. I am very moved by what you talked about and I cannot imagine the amount of luck that you must have had to be lucky enough to be one of five children that were ready to be shot to survive. That was without a doubt a miracle.

Ola

◇ ◇ ◇

Your father was a smart man to tell you to get out of the line to hide. It must be really hard to get up there and remember such horrible things. I'm really glad I got to hear your story. You are a very remarkable man to be able to get on stage and have such a positive attitude. I only hope the best for you.

Michelle

Meeting you made me feel lucky, because when I complain about things and get sad about things they usually are nothing compared to what you went through. I really think it is amazing that you lived through this and didn't hate the Germans or the Polish people.

Andy

After your presentation I felt so lucky to live in the United States.

Danielle

◇◇◇

I try not to think of myself having a worse life than someone else anymore because if I think about my childhood compared to your childhood, I actually have it pretty good.

Laura

◇◇◇

I think you are a very great man! You're such a great role model to people. You're a very nice man and also very funny. It is just so unbelievably great how you survived the holocaust from going through all the terrible obstacles through your life including some that would've led you to your death. It is just so amazing to me.

Hannah

◇◇◇

Thank you for coming to our school. I really learnt and now look at life different. Knowing that someone got a second chance at life makes me think I should take advantage of mine because we only live once and it's a gift to live. I really felt that pain but never could have lived through what you went through. Why because every day in my neighborhood I have friends getting killed by colors and sign. It hurts but I have to keep on going knowing I could be next. All those days you went through and made it out is really hope of life. It helps knowing you still got a smile and someone to love you. That's why I got to be someone in this world. Someday I look back at this and remember like you showed me hope is really there. Just look for it.

Jose

Thank You, Mr. Harris… Sincerely,

*The students and staff of Latino Youth High School and...
the students from many other schools...*

*Danusia, Julia, Juan, Will, Michael, Nick, Damaris,
Jackie, Jacob, Piper, Cam, Hailey, Alexa, Angelika,
Christine, Kimmy, Chelsie, Xavier, Heidi, Tierra, Monicah,
J.D., Jessica, Lisa, John. Eric, Lisa, Maria, M., Karen,
Nick, Morgan, Kelli, Ashley, Brian, Alex, Burt, Lindsey,
J.D., Dan, Ariel, Grace, Ryan, Mecti, Giovanni, Kienan,
Ellie, Pam, Amelia, Sarah, Amanda, Christina, Jackie,
J.D., Grace, Casey, Joey, David, Chuck, Jason, Donald,
Hannah, Jeremiah, Alex, Will, Karia, John, Lory, Yasmin,
J., Harrison, Bryce, Casey, Michael, Jon, Amanda, Chris,
Danny, Zeba, Laura, Jimmy, Tammy, Charlie, Andrea,
Aditi, Conner, D., Erik, Tyler, Gunnar, Cammeron, Burton,
Jeremy, Lauren, Allison, Alex, Yvonne, Celia, Sammie,
Stephanie, Ivan, Nick, Toni, M., D., David, Aldeu,
Martina, Maria, Adam, Dahlia, Samuel, Steve, Matthew,
Adam, Paola, Kirtan, Ramiro, Alex, Joanna, Kristina,
Carry, Rozzy, Eddie, Grace, Christian, Dylan, Min, Kim,
Jorge, Jenny, Rimantas, Jan, Ryan, Jason, Mayza, Michael,
Monike, John, Raven, Cate, Stephanie, Nakia, Kaitlin, Mo,
Lauren, Nikhil, Victor, Hasto, Jean-Luc, Daniel, Sarah,
Jon, Brett, Shelby, Ethan, Brayden, Addison, Joe, Reece,
Madeline, Dana, Amanda, Emma, Elliot, Chris, Danny,
Maddy, Jordan, Megan, Azra, Colleen, Brady, Taylor, Janae,
Jordon, Kash, Stephanie, Natalia, Emily, Mark, Peter, Ola,
Michelle, Andy, Danielle, Laura, Hannah, Jose.*

Conclusion

After hearing Sam Harris speak about his tragic losses and the horrific times he endured as a child, and realizing how he nevertheless emerged with abundant positivity instead of a habituated desire for revenge, students experience a change in their own perspectives on their lives. Many realize that their problems that had seemed insurmountable to them, are not that bad after all compared to those of the young Sammy's. Sam had overcome his problems and so could they. Sam is a happy, humorous, optimistic and caring person despite the emotional and physical suffering he had endured. Perhaps they, too, could have that positive outlook on life.

Yes, Sam is an inspiration to them. They call him *a role model, a hero, a legacy*. One student said in a letter, *you've got guts*. In another letter, a kid said, *you rock*. He also gives them practical advice when he tells them not to let bullies control their lives because bullies are really cowards who resort to physical or verbal abuse rather than have the courage to risk an even exchange—in case they lose. "So," he says, "You can stand up to bullies, too, and stop them in their tracks. Did you know that Hitler was the ultimate bully and people and nations were afraid to stand up to him?" Indeed, Hitler, who had ruled through coercion, intimidation, terrorization—and demonization—was **the ultimate bully**.

The students have learned important lessons about the Holocaust from Sam's *first account memory.* They realize how fortunate they are to live in the USA and intend not to take the country or their families for granted anymore. They feel grateful to have families or people upon whom they can rely. Sam's determination to survive—and thrive—impresses them and they are amazed at the fact that he does not hate or demonize a nation or people collectively.

The letters of the students are gems. Not only is the importance of Holocaust Education grasped, but they also have gained an understanding of what is true courage and what is cowardly bullying. *You are a strong man. The strongest man I ever knowed. You are a peaceful and humble man.* The students' empathetic capacity resonates throughout the letters. At times, they demonstrate their protective instincts towards Sam and also want to comfort him: *I would have peed in the bed too if all those bodies were there.* One kid feels both compassion and outrage: *There was NO REASON for what you had to face.* Another says, *I only wish I was there…I would have helped as much as I could. I just want to cry.* There is also incredulity: *I can't believe the horrors you had to go through.*

The students have learned a great deal about living a worthwhile, purposeful life from Sam and vow to remember their meeting with—as some have called him—*a great man.* They also realize how important it is to embrace opportunities. Various versions of the concept, ***If you can make it Mr. Harris…so can I,*** have become their mantra. How nice it is for the students to know that if they, too, are self-challenging—just like Sam—they can create their own positive path in life! It wasn't easy for Sam—yet, he made it. Therefore, so can they.

Through their letters, the students have allowed us to access their young minds, and we emerge with both a better understanding of their anxieties and an appreciation of their potential for true compassion. Sam has aroused the hearts of these kids. There is something poetic about the depths of their emotional experiences. I see these letters as their petition to us for help in ensuring that they can depend on the perpetuation of good values and positivity.